CW00420378

Victor Horta

Victor Horta

teNeues

Editor in chief:
Paco Asensio

Archipockets coordination:
Aurora Cuito

Editor and original texts:
María Sol Kliczkowski

Photographs:
© Christine Bastin, Jacques Evrard/
Ministère de la Région de Bruxelles-Capitale/Sofam
Photograph on page 6 © Musée Horta, Saint-Gilles/Sofam

English translation:
William Bain

German translation:
Oliver Herzig (Books Factory *Translations*)

French translation:
Agencia Lingo Sense

Italian translation:
Giovanna Carnevali

Graphic design / Layout:
Emma Termes Parera and Soti Mas-Bagà

Published worldwide by teNeues Publishing Group
(except Spain, Portugal and South-America):

teNeues Book Division
Kaistraße 18, 40221 Düsseldorf, Germany
Tel.: 0049-(0)211-994597-0
Fax: 0049-(0)211-994597 40

teNeues Publishing Company
16 West 22nd Street, New York, N.Y., 10010, USA
Tel.: 001-212-627-9090
Fax: 001-212-627-9511

teNeues Publishing UK Ltd.
Aldwych House, 81 Aldwych
London WC2B 4HP, UK
Tel.: 0044-1892-837-171
Fax: 0044-1892-837-272

teNeues France S.A.R.L.
140, rue de la Croix Nivert
75015 Paris, France
Tel.: 0033-1-5576-6205
Fax: 0033-1-5576-6419

www.teneues.com

Editorial project:

© 2003 LOFT Publications
Domènech 7-9, 2º 2ª
08012 Barcelona, Spain
Tel.: 0034 932 183 099
Fax: 0034 932 370 060
e-mail: loft@loftpublications.com
www.loftpublications.com

Printed by:
Gráficas Anman. Sabadell, Spain.

February 2003

Bibliographic information published by Die Deutsche Bibliothek
Die Deutsche Bibliothek lists this publication in the Deutsche Nationalbibliografie;
detailed bibliographic data is available in the Internet at http://dnb.ddb.de.

ISBN: 3-8238-5542-5

House of the people, Brussels, Belgium
Volkshaus, Brüssel, Belgien
Maison du Peuple, Bruxelles, Bélgique
Casa del Pòpolo, Brusselles, Belgio

One can affirm—offering examples such as the Paul Hankar House, the Old England store, or the Hanon House—that Brussels is outstanding for the wealth of Art Nouveau architecture that graces its streets. Victor Horta was one of the most interesting forerunners of this breakaway style, and he established a highly personal way of doing architecture.

Contrary to what is commonly believed, Art Nouveau did not limit itself to private residences of the rising bourgeoisie. In fact, other, institutional type buildings were also put up under the influence of this trend. It is in this sense that Horta will contribute with his architecture, raising structures like the Brugmann Hospital or the House of the People—no longer standing—a symbol of the moral and material solidarity linked to organized labor.

Unfortunately, the study of Horta's work is limited to the contemplation of his buildings themselves because in 1945, when he was changing residences, the greater part of his files was destroyed. But in spite of the scantiness of documentation, it is still possible to identify among the influences his master Alphonse Balat—the official architect of Leopold II—who for Horta constitutes the representative par excellence of the classical and rationalist paradigm. He would also experience a fascination for Poelaert, Garnier, and Viollet-le-Duc; from Eiffel he would take the use of iron and steel (for windows, stained-glass mounts, and skylights—all clear allusions to the French engineer's Eiffel tower).

However, Horta's great achievement was to free architecture from the guardianship of neo-Classical and Gothic lines to reinvent forms with greater freedom of expression and a more practical spirit. He will thus adapt architecture to real programs and express it by way of a very substantial array of materials which his times were placing at the disposal of the builder.

Under the aforementioned premises do we perceive the Tassel House, which conceives architecture with a new spirit in regard to material and which is considered to be the first of Belgium's Art Nouveau buildings.

While Victor Horta was well acquainted with the advantages the use of the curved line would bring him—it is attractive and dynamic, and expresses nuances—by comparison with the straight (and colder) line, all of his compositions would establish a balanced relationship between the two without ever breaking building imperatives. Additionally, owing to his exceptional imagination, he would constantly submit to renovation his own creative forms in order to adapt them to highly varied programs.

For Horta, each part of a work should be completed by another: the whole should link and adapt intimately the client's sensitivity. Sculptures, ornamental motifs, wrought iron work, moldings, stained glass, lighting systems, carpets, were all treated as independent entities and elevated to form part of a noble architecture. Horta never accepted the repetition of his creations, and extolled the originality of the elements themselves.

His elaborate system of work is reflected in the plans: the sections and elevations always translate rhythmic plans that maintain a formal balance and make evident the research time dedicated; each section is possessed of a detailed study of materials and of their relation to the work as a whole. Even when it is difficult for him to express in a drawing some of the innumerable details of stone, wood, iron, marble, or bronze, he will first order molds of plaster. From the beginning of his career, Horta was aware of the way beauty and originality are often born of solutions to specific problems, and this is why he often complicated his building details for the sake of achieving a more harmonious result.

Van Eetvelde House, Brussels, Belgium
Van Eetvelde Haus, Brüssel, Belgien
Maison Van Eetvelde, Bruxelles, Bélgique
Casa Van Eetvelde, Brusselles, Belgio

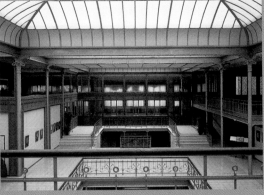

Waucquez Shopping Mall, Brussels, Belgium
Die großen Waucquez-Warenhäuser, Brüssel, Belgien
Grands magasins Waucquez, Bruxelles, Bélgique
Grandi magazzini Waucquez, Brusselles, Belgio

Anhand von Beispielen wie dem Paul-Hankar-Haus, dem Old-England-Lager oder dem Hanon-Haus kann man die These aufstellen, dass Brüssel sich durch die Art nouveau-Architektur in seinen Straßen auszeichnet. Victor Horta war einer der interessantesten Vorläufer dieses fragilen Stils und begründete eine sehr persönliche Form der Architektur.

Im Gegensatz zur gängigen Meinung beschränkte sich der Art nouveau nicht nur auf Privathäuser des entstehenden Bürgertums, sondern es wurden unter dem Einfluss dieser Strömung auch andere Gebäude von institutionellem Charakter gebaut. Horta trug mit seiner Architektur dazu bei, etwa durch das Brugmann-Krankenhaus oder auch mit dem nicht mehr erhaltenen Volkshaus, einem Symbol des mit der proletarischen Bewegung verbundenen moralischen und materiellen Gemeinschaftsgeistes.

Leider ist das Studium von Hortas Leistung auf die Betrachtung seiner Werke beschränkt, da er bei seinem Umzug 1945 große Teile seines Archivs zerstörte. Trotz der fehlenden Unterlagen ist besonders der Einfluss seines Meisters Alphonse Balat spürbar, offizieller Architekt von Leopold II, der für Horta die Perfektion des klassischen und rationalistischen Ideals repräsentierte. Auch von Poelaert, Garnier oder Viollet-le-Duc war er fasziniert, und von Eiffel übernahm er den Gebrauch von Eisen und Stahl – eine klare Anspielung auf die Ästhetik des Eiffelturms in seinen Glasfenstern, Glastüren und Dachluken.

Das große Verdienst Hortas war die Befreiung der Architektur von der Vorherrschaft neoklassischer und gotischer Linien, um die Formen mit größerer Freiheit und einem praktischen Geist neuzuerfinden. Er passte sie an reale Pläne an und verlieh ihnen durch die breite Palette der ihm zu Lebzeiten zur Verfügung stehenden Materialien Ausdruck. Diese Prämissen machen sich bemerkbar am Tassel-Haus, das die Architektur im Bezug auf Materialien neu definiert und als das erste belgische Art nouveau-Gebäude angesehen wird.

Obwohl Horta sich der Vorteile der Verwendung der gebogenen Linie, die attraktiv und dynamisch ist und den Ausdruck von Feinheiten erlaubt, gegenüber der geraden, kühleren bewusst war, fand er in all seinen Kompositionen eine ausgeglichene Relation zwischen beiden, ohne je gegen bauliche Anforderungen zu verstoßen. Außerdem waren durch seine außergewöhnliche Einfallsgabe seine Formen einer konstanten Veränderung unterworfen, um sie den verschiedensten Plänen anzupassen.

Für Horta musste jeder Teil eines Werkes durch einen anderen Teil vervollständigt werden: Alles musste vertrauensvoll miteinander kombiniert und an die Vorlieben seines Kunden angepasst werden. Skulpturen, verzierende Motive, geschmiedete Eisenarbeiten, dekorative Elemente, Fenster, Beleuchtung, Teppichböden wurden als unabhängige Einheiten angesehen und wurden zu Bestandteilen einer edlen Architektur erhoben. Nie akzeptierte er die Wiederholung seiner Schöpfungen und er predigte die Ursprünglichkeit seiner eigenen Elemente.

Sein ausgefeiltes Arbeitssystem zeigt sich in seinen Plänen: Schnitte und Aufrisse übersetzen immer rhythmische Pläne, die ein formales Gleichgewicht halten und die investierte Arbeitszeit durchscheinen lassen; jedem Schnitt ist eine detaillierte Studie der Materialien und ihres Verhältnisses zum Ganzen beigefügt. Wenn es sich als schwierig erwies, eine Zeichnung von einigen der unzähligen Details aus Stein, Holz, Eisen, Marmor oder Bronze anzufertigen, ordnete er sogar zuerst das Erstellen von Gipsmodellen an. Schon am Anfang seiner Karriere fand Horta heraus, dass Schönheit und Originalität oft aus der Lösung bestimmter Probleme resultierten, weshalb er oft bauliche Details mit dem Ziel, ein harmonischeres Resultat zu erreichen, verkomplizierte.

Brugmann Hospital, Brussels, Belgium
Das Brugmann–Krankenhaus, Brüssel, Belgien
Hôpital Brugmann, Bruxelles, Bélgique
Ospedale Brugmann, Brusselles, Belgio

Brugmann Hospital, Brussels, Belgium
Das Brugmann–Krankenhaus, Brüssel, Belgien
Hôpital Brugmann, Bruxelles, Bélgique
Ospedale Brugmann, Brusselles, Belgio

L'on peut affirmer – en prenant pour exemple la maison de Paul Hankar, les magasins Old England ou la maison Hanon – que Bruxelles est remarquable pour l'architecture Art Nouveau qui anime ses rues. Victor Horta fut l'un des plus intéressants précurseurs de ce style en rupture, établissant une forme très personnelle de création architecturale.

Contrairement à une croyance répandue, l'Art Nouveau ne s'est pas cantonné aux demeures particulières de la bourgeoisie naissante mais a également influencé la construction d'autres immeubles de caractère institutionnel. En ce sens, Horta pourra apporter sa contribution architecturale à des œuvres comme l'hôpital Brugmann ou la maison du Peuple – aujourd'hui disparue – symbole de la solidarité morale et matérielle liée à l'organisation prolétaire.

Malheureusement, l'étude de l'œuvre de Horta est limitée à la contemplation de ses travaux. En effet, lors de son déménagement en 1945, il détruisit en grande partie ses archives. En dépit de l'absence de documentation, il est possible d'identifier entre ses influences son maître, Alphonse Balat, architecte officiel de Léopold II, qui fut pour Horta le représentant de la perfection de l'idéal classique et rationnel. Il sera également fasciné par Poelaert, Garnier ou Viollet-le-Duc. D'Eiffel, il captera l'usage du fer et de l'acier qu'il emploiera pour ses fenêtres, verrières et claires-voies, en une allusion esthétique flagrante à la Tour Eiffel.

L'idée de génie de Horta fut de libérer l'architecture de la tutelle des lignes néoclassiques et gothiques, afin de réinventer les formes avec une plus grande liberté et un esprit pratique, de l'adapter à des projets réels et de l'exprimer au moyen d'un éventail substantiel de matériaux que l'époque mettait à sa disposition. C'est selon ces prémisses qu'il faut appréhender la maison Tassel – considérée comme le premier édifice Art Nouveau belge – concevant l'architecture avec un nouvel esprit, quant à l'emploi des matériaux.

Bien qu'il ait été au fait des avantages présentés par l'emploi de la ligne courbe – séduisante, dynamique et permettant d'exprimer les nuances – en regard de la ligne droite – plus froide – Horta établit dans toutes ses compositions une relation les équilibrant, sans jamais rompre avec les impératifs de construction. De plus, grâce à une imagination exceptionnelle, il soumet à une constante évolution ses formes créatives afin de les adapter aux programmes les plus variés.

Pour Horta, chaque partie d'une œuvre doit avoir son pendant : l'ensemble doit être intimement lié et adapté à la sensibilité du client. Sculptures, motifs ornementaux, travail du fer forgé, éléments décoratifs, verrières, illumination et tapis sont traités comme des entités indépendantes et élevés à former partie d'une architecture noble. Il n'accepta jamais la répétition de ses créations et prédit l'originalité des éléments propres.

Son système de travail, élaboré, se reflète dans ses plans : sections et élévations traduisent toujours des plans rythmiques maintenant un équilibre formel et révèlent le temps consacré à l'étude ; chaque partie affiche une étude détaillée des matériaux et de sa relation avec l'œuvre globale. Même lorsqu'il lui était difficile d'exprimer en un dessin certains des détails innombrables en pierre, bois, fer, marbre ou en bronze, il commandait tout d'abord des moulages en plâtre. Depuis les débuts de sa carrière, Horta fut conscient du fait que la beauté et l'originalité naissent fréquemment de la résolution de problèmes spécifiques. Pour cette raison, il compliquait souvent les détails de construction en vue d'atteindre un résultat plus harmonieux.

Tassel House, Brussels, Belgium
Tassel Haus, Brüssel, Belgien
Maison Tassel, Bruxelles, Bélgique
Casa Tassel, Brusselles, Belgio

Tassel House, Brussels, Belgium
Tassel Haus, Brüssel, Belgien
Maison Tassel, Bruxelles, Bélgique
Casa Tassel, Brusselles, Belgio

Se pensiamo alla casa di Paul Hankar, ai magazzini Old England o alla casa Hanon, si può certamente affermare che Brussselles è il punto di rifermento per l'architettura dell'Art Nouveau che caratterizza le sue strade. Victor Horta fu uno dei più interessanti precursori di questo esuberante stile, stabilì una forma molto personale di fare architettura.

Contrariamente a ciò che si pensa, l'Art Nouveau non si limitò nel creare residenze private della borghesia nascente, ma si caratterizza anche e sopratutto per tutti gli edifici di carattere istuzionaleche si costruirono sotto l'influsso di questa corrente. In quest'ottica Horta contribuirà, con la sua architettura, nel creare opere come l'ospedale Brugmann o la Casa del Pòpolo – oggi scomparsa, simbolo della solidarietà morale e materiale legata alla organizzazione proletaria.

Disgraziatamente, lo studio dei lavori di Horta è limitato alla contemplazione delle sue opere, infatti quando nel 1945 trasloca dal suo appartamento e distrugge gran parte dei suoi archivi. Non ostante la mancanza di documentazione, è tuttavia possibile identificare una delle sue influenze nella persona di Alphonse Balat – architetto ufficiale di Leopoldo II – che per Horta costituisce il rappresentante della perfezione dell'ideale classico e razionale. Verrà affasciato anche da Poelaert, Garnier o Viollet-le-Duc; e da Eiffel apprenderà l'utilizzo del ferro e dell'acciaio, che adopererà nelle vetrate, nei lucernari, nella chiara allusione estetica della Torre Eiffel.

Il grande successo del lavoro di Horta fu quello di liberare l'architettura dal controllo delle linee neoclassiche e gotiche per reinventare forme con maggiore libertà e spìrito pratico; adattarla a programmi reali ed esprimerla nei più svariati materiali che il costruttore di quell'epoca aveva a disposizione. Con queste premesse si può comprendere la casa Tassel, concepita con un nuovo spìrito nell'architettura grazie ai materiali utilizzati, ed è considerata il primo edificio dell'Art Nouveau belga.

Non ostante era a conoscenza dei vantaggi che gli recava l'utilizzo della lìnea curva – é attrattiva e dinamica e permette di definire i dettagli – rispetto alla lìnea retta – più fredda, Horta stabilisce in tutte le sue composizioni una equilibrata relazione tra le due, senza rompere assolutamente gli imperativi costruttivi. Inoltre, grazie alla sua eccezionale immaginazione, sottopone a costante rinnovamento le sue forme creative al fine di adattarle ai programmi più vari.

Per Horta, ciascuna parte di un'opera doveva essere contemplata dall'altra: tutto doveva essere intimamente legato e adattato alla sensibilità del proprio cliente. Sculturi, motivi ornamentali, lavori in ferro battuto, elementi decorati, vitrati, illuminazioni, tappeti, erano trattati come entità indipendenti e chiamati a fare parte di un'architettura nobile. Non accettò mai la ripetizione delle sue creazioni, e predicò l'originalità dei propri elementi.

Il suo sistema elaborato si riflette nei suoi piani: le sezioni e gli prospetti si traducono sempre in piani ritmici e mantengono un equilibrio formale e trasmettono il tempo dedicatoci nel realizzarli; ciascuna parte prevede uno studio dettagliato dei materiali e delle sue relazioni con il complesso. Anche quando gli risultava difficile esprimere in un disegno alcuni degli innumerevoli dettagli in pietra, legno, marmo o bronzo, ordinava anteriormente ad altre persone che realizzassero un modello in gesso. Sin dall'inizio della sua carriera professionale, Horta si rese conto che la bellezza e l'originalità nascono spesso de sollevare problemi specifici, grazie ai quali complicava i suoi dettagli costruttivi al fine di realizzare un risultato più armonioso.

Autrique House

Chaussée de Haecht 242, Brussels, Belgium
1893–1895

Horta enthusiastically accepted the commission of the construction of this home, his first such private residence, from an adept of Freemasonry from Brussels with whom the architect had begun a friendship. Built according to the traditional typology of the private dwelling, with three rooms arranged in a row, free of luxury and extravagance, this dwelling shows Horta's experimentation with some solutions that already announce the Tassel House, where he will clearly reveal his innovative style. Horta's imagination has left its mark in the façade, whose asymmetric composition highlights each aperture. On the top floor, the void of the gallery situated between two columns contributes to the dilation of the space. It is a distribution that comprises a chance bet in the face of the demands of the perpendicular correspondences of negative and positive spaces, of clerestory axes and walls lacking windows. The entire front is marked by the use of detail: granite wall decorations, curved cornice windows, the asymmetrical forms ... Horta's enthusiasm can even make him waive his fees just to be able to use white limestone in the façade—no doubt already over budget—a material which, combined with red stucco courses, creates a chic color contrast.

Horta nahm mit Begeisterung den Auftrag für sein erstes Privathaus von einem Angehörigen der Brüsseler Freimaurerloge an, mit dem er befreundet war. Gemäß der traditionellen Typologie eines Privathauses mit drei aneinander angrenzenden Räumen ohne Luxus und Extravaganzen versuchte sich Horta bei diesem Haus schon an einigen, das Tassel-Haus ankündigenden Lösungen, bei dem er definitiv Innovationen vorstellte. Seine Fantasie hinterließ Spuren an der Fassade, die in ihrer asymmetrischen Komposition jede Öffnung hervorhebt. Im letzten Stockwerk trägt die Lücke zwischen zwei Säulen der Galerie zur Ausweitung des Raumes bei. Diese Aufteilung stellt ein risikoreiches Unterfangen dar aufgrund der Anforderungen in der Vertikalen bezüglich Leere und Fülle sowie der Achsen zwischen Fenstern und Zonen ohne natürliches Licht. Die ganze Fassade zeichnet eine detaillierte Gestaltung aus: Mauerdekorationen aus Granit, Fenster mit Kurvenkranzgesimsen, asymmetrische Formen ... Die Begeisterung Hortas ging so weit, dass er auf sein Honorar verzichtete, um in der Fassade weißen Kalkstein benutzen zu können, der die vorgesehenen Kosten überstieg und in der Kombination mit Streifen von rotem Stuck einen eleganten farblichen Kontrast ergibt.

Horta accepte avec enthousiasme de construire sa première résidence particulière commandée par un franc-maçon bruxellois avec qui il avait entamé une relation d'amitié. Suivant la typologie traditionnelle de la résidence particulière, trois atmosphères se succédant à la file, sans luxe ni extravagance, Horta expérimente quelques solutions annonçant déjà la maison Tassel, où il révèlera enfin son caractère novateur. Son imagination laisse ses traces sur la façade, dont la composition asymétrique rehausse chaque ouverture. Au dernier étage, le vide de la galerie située entre les deux piliers contribue à dilater l'espace. Cette distribution constitue un pari risqué face à l'exigence des correspondances verticales de vides et de pleins, d'axes de fenêtre et de parois aveugles. Toute la façade est marquée par le traitement des détails : décorations murales en granit, corniches courbées des fenêtres, formes asymétriques... L'enthousiasme de Horta est tel qu'il renonce à ses honoraires pour pouvoir utiliser en façade une pierre blanche calcaire, hors budget – un matériau qui, allié aux bandes de stuc rouges, crée un élégant contraste chromatique.

Horta accetta con entusiasmo di costruire la sua prima residenza privata commissionatale da un iscritto alla framassoneria di Brusselles con cui aveva instaurato un rapporto di amicizia. Seguendo la tipologia tradizionale della casa privata, con tre ambienti disposti a schiera, senza alcun lusso e stravaganza, Horta sperimenta in questo progetto alcune soluzioni che anticipano la casa Tassel, dove rivelerà definitivamente il suo carattere innovatore. La sua immaginazione lascia il segno nella facciata, la cui composizione asimmetrica esalta ogni apertura. All'ultimo piano, il vuoto della galleria situata tra le due colonne, contribuisce nel dilatare lo spazio. Questa distribuzione costituisce una scommessa rischiosa di fronte all'esigenza delle corrispondenze verticali tra vuoti e pieni, tra assi delle finestre e cortine cieche. Tutta la facciata è segnata dal trattamento del dettaglio: decorazioni murali con granito, cornici curve di finestre, forme asimmetriche... L'entusiasmo di Horta arriva fino al punto di rinunciare al proprio onorario per poter realizzare una facciata in pietra bianca calcarea – già fuori dal preventivo prestabilito, un materiale che, combinato con strisce di stucco rosa, crea un elegante contrasto cromatico.

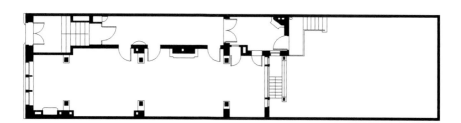

Plan
Grundriss
Niveau
Pianta

0 1 2

Tassel House

Rue Paul-Émile Janson 6, Brussels, Belgium
1893–1895

Autrique House had still not been completed when another of the architect's friends, the geometry teacher Tassel, decided to commission Horta with a new piece. The narrowness and the depth of the terrain as well as the height that would be required of the construction were not easy requisites to fulfill. But Horta managed to make this structure stand out among the rest with a great freedom of forms. The symmetry planned by the architect is reflected in the façade, whose central element is a bow window in the ochre and blue stone that is such a characteristic part of Horta's works. The cornice over the entrance constitutes the composition's figurative support. And yet it is this central bow window that brings across the architect's mastery, rejecting all stylistic artifice. On the iron railing, a highly dynamic touch, the decorative stone element is placed, giving the metallic forms greater solidity. The composition unites all of the themes of Horta's language: the relation between structure and ornament, continuity, discontinuity, coordination of materials ... And the symmetry is precisely what resolves the exploration and resolution of the project.

Das Autrique-Haus war noch nicht vollendet, als sich ein weiterer Freund Hortas, der Geometrielehrer Tassel, dazu entschied, ihm den Auftrag eines neuen Gebäudes zu erteilen. Die Enge und Tiefe des Grundstücks sowie die Höhe, die das Gebäude erreichen sollte, waren schwierige Bedingungen; Horta schaffte es jedoch, die anderen mit großer Formenfreiheit zu übertreffen. Die vom Architekten entworfene Symmetrie spiegelt sich in der Fassade wider, welche als Hauptelement ein verglastes, sogenanntes „bow window" mit Rundbogen hat, das mit den für die Werke Hortas typischen ockerfarbigen und blauen Steinen verziert ist. Das Kranzgesims über dem Eingang unterstützt die Gesamtkomposition. Zweifellos jedoch ist es das zentrale „bow window", das die Meisterschaft des Architekten zur Geltung bringt und alle stilistischen Kunstfertigkeiten zurückweist. In der Balustrade aus Eisen, die eine starke Dynamik ausstrahlt, fügt sich ein dekoratives Steinelement ein, welches der Eisenform eine gewisse Festigkeit gibt. Diese Komposition vereinigt alle Themen der Sprache Hortas: Die Verbindung zwischen Struktur und Dekoration, Kontinuität und Unstetigkeit, das Zusammenspiel von Materialien ... Und es ist gerade die Symmetrie, welche die Erforschung und Lösung des Projektes vereinfacht.

La maison Autrique n'était pas encore terminée lorsque l'un de ses amis, le professeur de géométrie Tassel, décida de commander à Horta une nouvelle construction. L'étroitesse et la profondeur du terrain, comme la hauteur que devait atteindre la construction, étaient des impératifs difficiles à respecter. Pour autant, Horta réussit à le mettre en valeur grâce à une grande liberté formelle. La symétrie proposée par l'architecte se reflète sur la façade, dont l'élément central est une « bow window », une fenêtre arquée, qui se conjugue avec la pierre ocre et bleue caractéristique des œuvres de Horta. La corniche, située au-dessus de l'entrée, offre un support figuratif à la composition. Cependant, c'est la « bow window » centrale qui affirme la maîtrise de l'architecte, rejetant tous les artifices stylistiques. Pour la balustrade en fer, au dynamisme prononcé, est introduit un élément décoratif en pierre, apportant une certaine solidité aux formes métalliques. Cette composition réunit tous les thèmes du langage de Horta : relation entre la structure et la décoration, continuité, discontinuité, conjonction de matériaux... et c'est précisément la symétrie qui facilite l'exploration et donne la clé du projet.

La casa Autrique non si era ancora conclusa quando un altro dei suoi amici, il professore di geometria Tassel, decise di affidare a Horta un nuovo edificio. La strettezza e la profondità del terreno, così come l'altezza che l'edificio doveva raggiungere, erano requisiti difficili da compiere; tuttavia Horta riesce realizzarli con grande facilità di forme. La simmetria pensata dall'architetto si riflette nella facciata, il cui elemento centrale è una "bow window" in arco vetrata che si congiunge con la pietra di color ocra e azzuro caratteristica dei lavori di Horta. La cornice situata sopra l'entrata costituisce il supporto figurativo della composizione. Tuttavia, è proprio la "bow window" centrale l'elemento che afferma la maestrìa dell'architetto e che rifiuta tutto l'artificio stilistico. Nella balaustra in ferro, di grande dinamismo, si introduce un elemento decorativo della pietra, che conferisce solidità alle forme metalliche. Questa composizione raduna tutti i temi del linguaggio di Horta: relazione tra struttura e decorazione, continuità, discontinuità, insieme dei materiali... ed è precisamente la simmetria che facilita l'esplorazione e la risoluzione del progetto.

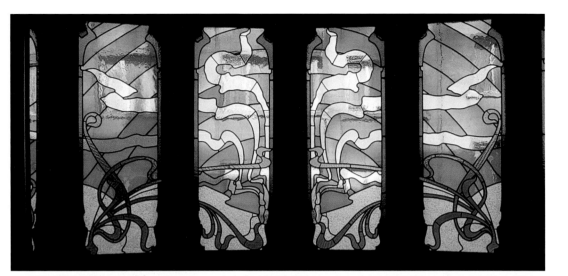

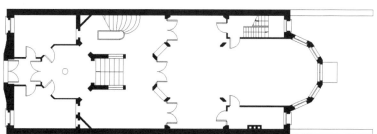

Plan
Grundriss
Niveau
Pianta

0 1 2

Winssinger House

Rue de l'Hôtel des Monnaies 66, Brussels, Belgium
1894–1896

The house of Winssinger, the engineer, had to satisfy the needs of his wife, incapacitated by long-term illness. Thus, Horta designed an arrangement conditioned to guarantee repose and quiet. In the layout of the façade, he returns to the idea of symmetry and introduces, based on a quadripartite design, a bow window that emerges from the wall decoration in such a way as to shape the vertical axis dominating the whole. It thus works as an interface for the two first-floor balconies. Two columns of Gothic stamp define this salient curve, while four slender steel ones divide it vertically to serve as supports for the upper balcony. The ground floor and the mezzanine were used as public, family spaces and are closely linked and magnificently appointed. Each component has been closely studied in relation to its accompanying elements, thus showing the respect Horta gave to simple, unadorned habitations. In much the same way, the interior stairway, with its riveted and varnished columns and a light railing, demonstrates the way in which the artist would extol the deep meaning of both structure and space in his pieces.

Das Haus des Ingenieurs Winssinger musste den Erfordernissen gerecht werden, die die Krankheit seiner Ehefrau mit sich brachte, so dass Horta eine Aufteilung entwarf, die Ruhe und Erholung gewährleistete. Bei der Komposition der Fassade kehrte er zum Thema „Symmetrie" zurück und fügte ein auf einem vierteiligen Rhythmus basierendes „bow window" ein, welches aus der Mauerverzierung hervortritt und eine das ganze Gebäude dominierende vertikale Achse sowie eine Verbindung mit den beiden Balkonen des ersten Stocks bildet. Zwei gotisch anmutende Säulen umranden den geschwungenen, hervorgehobenen Part, während vier feine Eisenstützen sie vertikal durchqueren, um so den darüber liegenden Balkon zu festigen. Das Erdgeschoss und das Souterrain waren für das gesellschaftliche Leben der Familie reserviert und beherbergen deutlich gegliederte, mit reicher Pracht dekorierte Räume. Jede Komponente wurde unter dem Blickwinkel der anderen Elemente bedacht und zeigt Hortas Respekt vor einfachen, ungekünstelten Strukturen. Auf die gleiche Weise zeigt die Innentreppe, welche aus eingefassten lackierten Wandpfeilern und einem leichten Geländer besteht, die Zielsetzung des Künstlers, den tieferen Sinn von Struktur und Raum zu betonen.

La maison de l'ingénieur Winssinger devait répondre aux exigences d'une épouse malade et ainsi, Horta put prévoir une distribution destinée à garantir le repos et la tranquillité. Dans la composition de la façade, il revient au thème de la symétrie et introduit, en se fondant sur un rythme à quatre temps, une « bow window » qui émerge du visage mural pour former un axe vertical dominant l'ensemble tout en fonctionnant comme un trait d'union entre les deux balcons du premier étage. Deux colonnes aux réminiscences gothiques encadrent cette courbure saillante, alors que quatre piliers métalliques affinés la traversent verticalement pour supporter le balcon supérieur. Le rez-de-chaussée et l'entresol sont réservés à la vie publique de la famille et proposent des espaces très articulés et décorés avec magnificence. Chaque composant a été étudié en fonction des éléments qui l'accompagnent et soulignent le respect de Horta pour les structures simples, dépourvues d'artifices. De la même manière, l'escalier intérieur, composé de pilastres rivetés et vernis et d'une fine balustrade, révèlent l'idée de l'artiste : ennoblir la signification profonde de la structure et de l'espace.

La casa dell'ingegnere Winssinger doveva soddifare le necessità della sua sposa ammalata, per cui Horta disegnò una distribuzione condizionata nel garantire il riposo e tranquillità. Nella composizione della facciata torna il tema della simmetria, e introduce, basandosi sul ritmo quadripartito, una "bow window" che emerge dal paramento murale e forma un asse verticale che domina il complesso e che funziona come un'unione dei due balconi del primo piano. Due colonne di reminiscenza gotica marcano questa curva, mentre quattro esili colonne di ferro lo attraversano verticalmente per esercitare la funzione di sostegno del balcone superiore. Il piano terra e il mezzanino erano destinati alla vita pubblica della famiglia e creano spazi articolati e decorati con magnificenza. Ciascun componente è estato studiato in funzione degli elementi che lo accompagnano e mostrano il rispetto di Horta nei confronti delle strutture semplici, senza artificio. Allo stesso modo, la scala interna, composta da pilastri bordati e verniciati e da una balaustra leggera, dimostra l'idea dell'artista nell'instaurare un significato profondo della struttura e dello spazio.

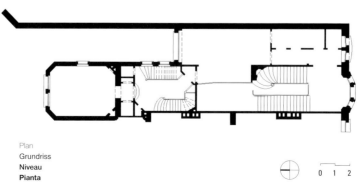

Plan
Grundriss
Niveau
Pianta

0 1 2

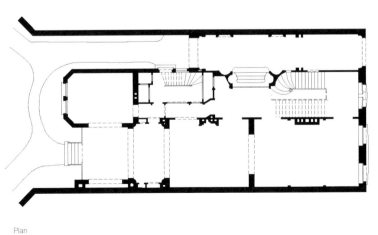

Plan
Grundriss
Niveau
Pianta

0 1 2

Solvay House

Avenue Louise 224, Brussel, Belgium
1894–1898

The success enjoyed by the company of Ernest Solvay between 1870 and 1880 reached global dimensions. His excellent financial place brought this engineer to solicit the services of Horta, the most expensive architect in the city, to build his personal residence. While the façade has been slightly modified, the arrangement in the interior, including the original furniture, has not changed. This large private home stands out for the control of the balance of its interior space, the dialogue between crafted elements and materials, and the symmetry of the façade. The whole reflects a synthesis of Horta's recurrent themes: curved walls, a combination of stone and iron, two-tone decoration, a rhythmical complexity ... The natural lighting, brought in through the glass of the roof, greatly amplifies the space. The ventilators of the façade reflect the importance granted to fresh air in the house. All of the elements of the interior architecture, including a double staircase with a gilt metal railing, were carefully designed by Horta himself. The warm colors conflate with the gilt, with the repeated motif of spirals in the marquetry and in the carpets to achieve a decoration of great preciosity.

Der Erfolg des Unternehmens von Ernest Solvay erreichte zwischen 1870 und 1880 eine weltweite Dimension. Seine daraus resultierende vortreffliche finanzielle Situation erlaubte dem Ingenieur, die Leistungen von Horta, dem damals teuersten Architekten der Stadt, für den Bau seines Privathauses in Anspruch zu nehmen. Obwohl die Fassade leicht verändert wurde, sind innere Anordung und Originalmöbel erhalten und intakt. Diese großzügige private Residenz besticht durch das Gleichgewicht im Innenraum, den Dialog zwischen Elementen und Material und seine symmetrische Fassade. Diese Einheit spiegelt eine Synthese der von Horta angewandten Themen wider: geschwungene Mauern, die Kombination von Eisen und Stein, zweifarbige Verzierungen, rhythmische Geschlossenheit ... Die natürliche Beleuchtung durch das Glasdach unterstreicht die Größe des Raumes. Die Lüftungsanlagen in der Fassade betonen die Wichtigkeit der Belüftung des Hauses. Alle Elemente der Innenarchitektur, zu der auch eine doppelte Treppe mit vergoldetem Geländer zählt, wurden auf liebevolle Art und Weise von Horta entworfen. Die warmen Farben mischen sich mit dem vergoldeten und mit dem sich wiederholenden Spiel aus Schneckenformen in Intarsien und Teppichboden, um so eine Dekoration in sehr preziösem Stil zu erreichen.

Le succès de l'entreprise d'Ernest Solvay atteint entre 1870 et 1880 une dimension mondiale. Sa situation économique florissante amène l'ingénieur à solliciter les services de Horta, l'architecte le plus cher de la ville, pour construire sa résidence particulière. Bien que la façade ait été légèrement modifiée, la disposition intérieure et les meubles d'origine ont été préservés intacts. Cette demeure privée aux dimensions conséquentes est remarquable de par le contrôle de l'équilibre de l'espace intérieur, le dialogue éléments – matériaux et la symétrie de la façade. L'ensemble reflète une synthèse des thèmes récurrents chez Horta : parois courbes, mariage de la pierre et du fer, parements bicolores, complexité rythmique... L'illumination naturelle, provenant de la verrière du toit, confère une grande amplitude à l'espace. Les bouches de ventilations de la façade reflètent l'importance attribuée à l'aération de la maison. Tous les éléments d'architecture intérieure, parmi lesquels un double escalier doté d'une balustrade en métal doré, ont été soigneusement conçus par Horta. Les couleurs chaudes se mêlent au doré, avec le jeu répétitif des spirales dans la marqueterie et dans les tapis, afin d'obtenir une décoration d'un réel raffinement.

Il successo che vive la compagnia di Ernest Solvay raggiunge tra il 1870 e il 1880 una dimensione mondiale. La sua eccellente situazione economica porta questo ingenere a chiedere una consulenza ad Horta, l'architetto più caro della città, per realizzare la sua casa privata. Anche se la facciata venne leggermente modificata, la disposizione interna ed i mobili originali si sono conservati intatti. Questa residenza privata di grandi dimensioni si distacca per il controllo dell'equilibrio dello spazio interno, il dialogo tra gli elementi e i materiali, e la simmetria della facciata. Il complesso riflette una sintesi dei temi ricorrenti di Horta: muri curvi, combinazioni di pietra e ferro, paramenti bicolori, complessità ritmica... L'illuminazione naturale, proveniente dalla vetrata del tetto, ingrandisce lo spazio. Le prese d'aria riflettono l'importanza attribuita all'aerazione della casa. Tutti gli elementi dell'architettura interna, tra cui si considera anche una doppia scala con balaustra in metallo dorato, furono accuratamente disegnati da Horta. I colori caldi si mescolano con il dorato, con il gioco ripetuto di spirali nelle stanze dei modelli e nei tappeti per raggiungere una decorazione di grande prestigio.

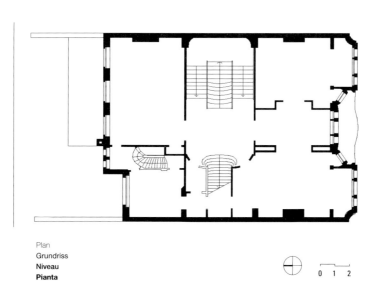

Plan
Grundriss
Niveau
Pianta

0 1 2

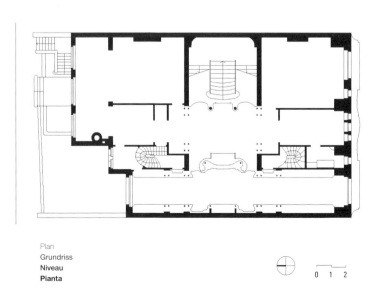

0 1 2

Van Eetvelde House

Avenue Palmerston 2-4, Brussels, Belgium
1895–1897 / 1898–1901

Although up to this time the use of iron had been reserved to industrial construction, Horta, the author of the novel fashion of Art Nouveau, will design an iron façade for this manor house commissioned by Edmond van Eetvelde. The architect proposes an innovative spatial arrangement: five parts structured on a diagonal plan that confer on motion the role of the program's generating element. A high number of decorative elements show the virtuosity with which Horta designed the interiors, always leaving the framing revealed and enriching them through the use of curved form. After the acquisition of the two adjacent terrains, Horta was called back to carry out an amplification. In contrast to what had been planned for the first building, he designed a stone façade, a change that points up the sculptural mode of Horta's language. The ensemble of the three buildings is brought about by a stone mounting that absorbs the pre-existing bow window and that serves the new entrance well. Inside, the use of materials as disparate as marble, wood or bronze stands out to the viewer's eye, as does the coexistence of forms used to achieve overall harmony.

Obwohl bis zu diesem Zeitpunkt der Gebrauch von Eisen dem Bau von Industriegebäuden vorbehalten war, entwarf Horta als Urheber des neuen Art nouveau-Stils für dieses von Edmond van Eetvelde in Auftrag gegebene Herrenhaus eine Eisenfassade. Der Architekt sah eine außergewöhnliche Strukturierung der Fassade in fünf Teile vor, gebaut auf einem diagonalen Grundstück – eine Gestaltung, die Bewegung als das den Gesamtplan konstituierende Element ausweist. Eine große Anzahl dekorativer Komponenten zeigt die Virtuosität, mit der Horta das Innere ausschmückte, wobei er immer die Strukturen sichtbar werden ließ und sie mit seinen geschwungenen Formen anreicherte. Nach dem Kauf der zwei anliegenden Grundstücke wurde Horta wieder beauftragt, um eine Erweiterung in Angriff zu nehmen. Im Gegensatz zu seinen Plänen für das erste Gebäude entwarf er diesmal eine Steinfassade, eine Veränderung, die die bildhauerischen Fähigkeiten Hortas zeigt. Die Verbindung der drei Gebäude wurde durch einen Steinbalken verwirklicht, welcher das Bogenfenster des bereits existierenden Gebäudes in sich aufnimmt und mit dem neuen Eingang verschmilzt. Im Inneren ist die Verwendung so ungleicher Materialien wie Marmor, Holz oder Bronze auffällig, aber auch das Nebeneinander von Formen, durch das eine absolute Harmonie des Ganzen erreicht wird.

Bien que l'emploi du fer ait été jusqu'alors réservé à la construction industrielle, Horta, artisan de la nouvelle mode de l'Art Nouveau, va concevoir une façade en fer pour cette demeure seigneuriale commandée par Edmond van Eetvelde. L'architecte suggère une disposition spatiale novatrice : cinq parties structurées selon un tracé diagonal confèrent au mouvement le rôle d'élément moteur du projet. Un nombre élevé d'éléments décoratifs affirme la virtuosité avec laquelle Horta habille les intérieurs, laissant toujours les structures apparaître pour les enrichir de formes courbes. Après l'acquisition des deux terrains adjacents, Horta est rappelé afin de réaliser une extension. Contrairement à ses projets pour le premier bâtiment, il conçoit une façade en pierre, un changement qui indique la tendance sculpturale du langage de Horta. L'assemblage des trois constructions est matérialisé au moyen d'un montant de pierre qui absorbe la « bow window » de l'édifice préexistant pour se conjuguer avec la nouvelle entrée. À l'intérieur devient notable l'emploi des matériaux aussi dissemblables que le marbre, le bois ou le bronze, mais aussi la coexistence de formes qui matérialisent une harmonie complète de l'ensemble.

Anche se fino al momento dell'utilizzazione del ferro si era dedicato alla costruzione industriale, Horta, artefice della nuova moda dell'Art Nouveau, disegnerà una facciata in ferro per questa casa signorile incaricata da Edmond van Eetvelde. L'architetto propone una disposizione spaziale innovatrice: cinque parti strutturali e un tracciato diagonale che conferisce al movimento il ruolo di elemento generatore del programma. Un elevato numero di elementi decorativi mostrano il virtuosismo con cui Horta trattò suoi interni, lasciando sempre le strutture a vista e arricchite con nuove curve. Con l'aquisizione dei due terreni adiacenti, Horta viene chiamato nuovamente per fare un'ampliamento. Contrariamente a quello previsto nel primo edificio, disegna una facciata in pietra che assorbe la "bow window" dell'edificio presistente e si relaziona con la nuova entrata. L'interno si distacca grazie all'utilizzo dei materi tra loro differenti come il marmo, il legno od il bronzo, così come la consistenza delle forme che raggiungono un'armonia totale del complesso.

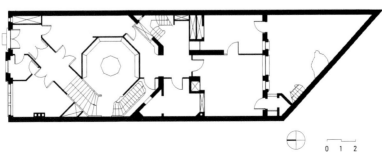

Plan
Grundriss
Niveau
Pianta

0 1 2

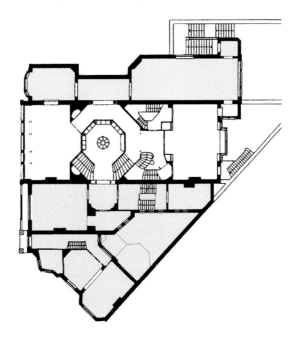

Plan
Grundriss
Niveau
Pianta

  0 1 2

Deprez House

Avenue Palmerston 3, Brussels, Belgium
1895-1897

In 1895, an important industrialist from Liège, Georges Deprez, commissioned Victor Horta to build a house to be used as an occasional residence in Brussels. This luxurious home was later extended and modified by Horta himself, in an intervention that broke up the unity of the composition and completely transformed the interiors. Following the renovation, the building acquired a more prudent and austere look than the original version. This project especially interested the architect because of the angularity of the edifice, its reduced dimensions, and the nearly complete absence of garden. The façade that gives onto Palmerston Avenue displays a great vivacity of expression, but the asymmetric rhythm was interrupted after the refurbishment project. As for the Bodougnat Street front, while much of its dynamic and variety has been lost, the details that originate from the hand of Horta can still be appreciated, such as the cornice over the door, in skillfully executed curves. Another salient point is the building's chimneys, which aesthetically close the construction. Still another is the colored stones, which alternate to accentuate the importance of certain angles or cornices.

1895 beauftragte ein wichtiger Industrieller aus Lüttich, Georges Deprez, Victor Horta mit dem Bau eines Hauses, um bei seinen kürzeren Aufenthalten in der Stadt eine Wohnung zu haben. Dieses luxuriöse Gebäude wurde später durch Horta selbst mittels eines Eingriffes vergrößert und verändert, der es seiner Ausgewogenheit beraubte und sein Inneres komplett verwandelte. Das Gebäude erhielt nun ein strengeres und zurückhaltenderes Äußeres als der ursprüngliche Bau. Dieses Projekt interessierte den Architekten vor allem, weil es sich um ein Eckgebäude handelte, das von geringer Dimension war und praktisch keinen Garten besaß. Die zur Avenue Palmerston hinausgehende Fassade drückt eine große Lebendigkeit aus, auch wenn ihr asymmetrischer Rhythmus bei der Erweiterung zerstört wurde. Bei der zur Rue Bodougnat hinausgehenden Fassade kann man, auch wenn sie viel von ihrer Vielfältigkeit und Kraft verloren hat, noch Details aus Hortas Hand bewundern, wie beispielsweise die mit geschickt geschwungenen Linien ausgestattete Auskragung, die sich über der Tür befindet. Man sollte auch auf die Kamine hinweisen, die das Gebäude ästhetisch vervollständigen, sowie auf die unterschiedliche Färbung der Steine, um die Wichtigkeit von bestimmten Winkeln und Ausbuchtungen zu unterstreichen.

En 1895, un important industriel liégeois, Georges Deprez, commande à Victor Horta une maison afin de disposer d'une résidence de passage à Bruxelles. Cette construction luxueuse fut, par la suite, agrandie et modifiée par Horta lui-même, en une intervention qui la déposséda de son unité de composition et transforma complètement ses intérieurs pour lui conférer un aspect plus prudent et austère que l'original. Ce projet intéressait particulièrement l'architecte car s'agissant d'un bâtiment en angle, mais aussi de par ses dimensions réduites et la quasi-absence de jardin. La façade donnant sur l'avenue Palmerston affiche une grande vivacité d'expression, bien que son rythme asymétrique soit rompu après la réforme. Sur la façade de la rue Bodougnat, et bien qu'elle ait perdu en vigueur et en variété, il est encore possible d'admirer des détails de la main d'Horta, ainsi l'encorbellement situé au-dessus de la porte, aux lignes courbes si délicates. Il convient également de signaler les cheminées, qui complètent esthétiquement l'édifice, sans oublier le jeu des couleurs de la pierre, en alternance afin de souligner l'importance de certains angles ou saillies.

Nel 1895, un importante industriale di Liegi, Georges Deprez, incarica a Victor Horta una casa al fine di avere a disposizione una residenza nelle vicinande di Brusselles: Questo edificio venne ampliato successivamente e modificato dallo stesso Horta, in un lavoro che gli spossessò da la sua unità compositiva e che trasformò completamente gli interni, ma che gli permesse di acquisire un aspetto più prudente austero rispetto all'originale. Questo progetto interessa specialmente l'architetto perchè si tratta di un edificio d'angolo, per le sue ridotte dimensioni e perchè risulta essere praticamente privo di giardino. La facciata che si affaccia sull'Avenida Palmerston dimostra una grande capacità espressiva, anche il su ritmo asimmetrico si romperà a causa della sua ampliazione. Sulla facciata della strada Bodougnat, non ostante abbia ormai perso molto del suo vigore e varietà, si possono ammirare tuttavia dettagli della mano di Horta, come per esempio l'aggetto che si trova sopra la porta, di linee curve. Ci sono da segnalare inoltre i camini, che completano esteticamente l'edificio, così come il gioco del colore della pietra, che si alterna per sottolineare l'importanza di certi angoli e di certi aggetti.

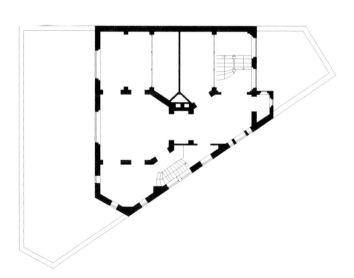

Plan
Grundriss
Niveau
Pianta

0　1　2

Horta Studio
(Horta Museum)

Rue Américaine 23-25, Brussels, Belgium
1898–1901

In 1898, Horta, then at the height of his career, acquired two adjacent plots to construct his own house and studio. His intention was to establish a clear distinction between the spaces, something which is perceived visually from the exterior, and to differentiate in this way the different uses that each area would serve. The studio opens out to the exterior thanks to its large apertures: on the first floor, a slender iron pier on a curved stone base supports a lowered double arch; on the second, the division is tripartite, setting up the superimposition of rhythms that culminate in the top-level arched clerestories. Bow windows dominate the façade in the private dwelling, with double windows crowned by an ironwork grille with rich ornamentation evocative of the wings of a butterfly. In the interior, the wooden staircase extends the perspective of the space, opening out slowly as it goes up. The helicoidal line is crowned by a large stained glass window that conflates the curved and the straight lines. At present the building serves as the Horta Museum, having undergone a careful and thorough restoration.

Im Jahre 1898 erwarb Horta auf dem Zenit seiner Karriere zwei nebeneinander liegende Grundstücke, um seine eigene Werkstatt und sein Wohnhaus zu errichten. Seine Intention war die klare Trennung zwischen Wohn- und Arbeitsraum, die man schon von außen wahrnimmt. Das Atelier öffnet sich dank seiner großzügigen Fenster nach außen: Im ersten Stock ruht ein feiner Eisenpfeiler auf einem geschwungenen Steinsockel, um einen doppelten abgesenkten Bogen zu unterstützen; im zweiten Stock teilt sich ein großräumiges Fenster in drei Abschnitte, was zu einer Überschneidung der Rhythmen beiträgt, die in den Öffnungen des letzten Stockwerks gipfelt. Doppelte Bogenfenster dominieren die Fassade des privaten Wohnhauses, die als Krönung von einer Balustrade, die in ihrer reichen Verzierung die Flügel eines Schmetterlings nachempfindet, geschmückt wird. Im Inneren erweckt eine Holztreppe den Eindruck, dass mehr Raum gewonnen wird, da sie nach oben hin schmaler wird. Ihre schneckenhafte Form wird von einem Fenster abgeschlossen, welches gerade und geschwungene Linien kombiniert. Zur Zeit wird das Horta-Museum dort beherbergt und aufgrund dessen wurde das Gebäude einer sorgfältigen Renovierung unterzogen.

En 1898, Horta, à l'apogée de sa carrière, fait l'acquisition de deux parcelles adjacentes afin d'établir sa propre demeure et son atelier. Il a dans l'intention d'énoncer une distinction claire entre les espaces, un élément perceptible visuellement depuis l'extérieur, et de différencier ainsi les fonctions variées que chaque partie doit remplir. L'atelier est ouvert sur l'extérieur grâce à de vastes fenêtres : au premier étage, un fin pilier de fer s'appuie sur un support en pierre aux formes courbes afin de soutenir un arc double abaissé ; au deuxième étage, le fenêtrage se divise en trois sections, ce qui contribue à une superposition de rythmes qui culmine avec les ouvertures du dernier niveau. Unes « bow windows » dominent la façade de la résidence privée, dotée de doubles fenêtres couronnées d'une balustrade dont la riche ornementation évoque les ailes d'un papillon. À l'intérieur, l'escalier de bois élargit la perception de l'espace en s'étrécissant peu à peu avec l'ascension. Son tracé hélicoïdal est coiffé d'une verrière qui combine les lignes droites et courbes. L'édifice accueille actuellement le Musée Horta, ce qui a impliqué une restauration soigneuse.

Nel 1898 Horta, all'apogeo della sua carriera, acquisisce due lotti adiacenti l'uno all'altro per costruire la propria abitazione e studio. La sua intenzione era quella di stabilire una chiara distinzione tra i differenti spazi, volontà questa che si percepisce visivamente dall'esterno, e differenziare in questo modo le differenti funzioni che ogni ambiente doveva assolvere. Lo studio si apre verso l'esterno grazie a delle ampie finestre: al primo piano, uno snello pilastro di ferro appoggia su un supporto di pietra di forma plastica per sorreggere un doppio arco ribassato; al secondo, invece, il ventanale si divide in tre parti, contribuendo ad una sovrapposizione dei ritmi che culmina nelle bucature dell'ultimo livello. "Bow windows" dominan la facciata dell'appartamento privato, con finestre doppie coronate da una balaustrata la cui ricca decorazione evoca le ali di una farfalla. All'interno, la scala di legno ingrandisce la visione dello spazio, restringendosi arbitrariamente mano a mano che sale. Il suo andamento elicoidale viene ripreso dalla cortina vetrata, che armonizza linee rette e curve. Attualmente accoglie il Museo Horta, destinazione in funzione della quale l'edificio venne sottoposto ad un rigoroso restauro.

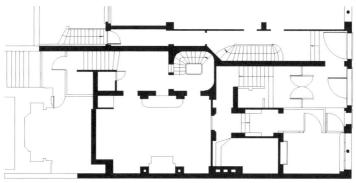

Plan
Grundriss
Niveau
Pianta

0 1 2

Max Hallet House

Avenue Louise 346, Brussels, Belgium
1903-1905

The mundane demands of the political office that occupied the owner of this house (who was also a lawyer) led him to ask Horta to be insistent in regard to his home's private interests. The white limestone façade boasts a compositional scheme in which the horizontal predominates, a ploy that confers a static balance. The back façade, as well, exhibits great imaginative exuberance on the part of the architect. It was conceived with great coherence and careful rationalism. These aspects are appreciable in the skillful solution given the small stairs that provide illumination for the basement. But here we also discover a Horta of something verging on almost Futurist imagination: the design, with a nod to science fiction, of the windows that stand out in the upper floor bow window. In the interior, one of the outstanding elements must be the staircase. It is perhaps the dominant key that structures the entire construction. The problem of heating was solved by way of a design that includes a series of very unique radiators that run along the windows. In this interplay of light, forms, and transparency, the architect may be seen to predate the Futurist movement in a singular and very pure use of space.

Aus dem repräsentativen Anspruch, den das Amt eines Politikers für den Besitzer dieses Hauses mit sich brachte, folgte, dass der Rechtsanwalt Horta zur Bedingung machte, dass das Gebäude seine Privatsphäre schützen müsse. Die Fassade aus weißem Kalkstein präsentiert ein Kompositionsschema, in dem die horizontalen Linien überwiegen, was ihr ein statisches Gleichgewicht verleiht. Auch die rückwärtige Fassade zeigt den Fantasiereichtum des Architekten. Ihr wurde eine große Einheitlichkeit und strenge Vernunft zugedacht, wie man es normalerweise an seiner Gestaltung der kleinen Kellerlichtschächte schätzt. Aber man entdeckt auch einen Horta mit fast futuristischer Fantasie, der den verglasten Fenstern über dem Bogenfenster galaktische Formen gab. Das Innere zeichnet sich durch eine Treppe aus, die das zentrale Element bildet, das die Konstruktion gliedert. Das Problem der Heizung wird mittels eines Entwurfs einzelner Radiatoren entlang der Fenster gelöst. Mit einem Spiel aus Licht, Formen und Transparenzen greift der Architekt auf einzigartige, puristische Weise der futuristischen Bewegung vor.

Les exigences mondaines d'une charge politique occupant le propriétaire de cette maison ont fait que cet avocat ait requis de Horta de préserver son intimité. La façade, en pierre calcaire blanche, présente un plan de composition où s'imposent les lignes horizontales qui lui confèrent son équilibre statique. Cependant, la façade postérieure fait preuve d'une imagination exubérante de la part de l'architecte. Elle fut conçue avec une grande cohérence et un rationalisme rigoureux, comme il est notable dans la solution apportée avec habileté aux petits escaliers, permettant le passage de la lumière dans la cave. Mais l'on découvre aussi un Horta à la fantaisie quasi-futuriste créant des fenêtres vitrées aux formes galactiques, se détachant sur la « bow window ». De l'intérieur, il faut remarquer l'escalier – un élément dominant et structurant la construction. La question du chauffage est résolue à l'aide radiateurs singuliers suivant la planimétrie des fenêtres. Dans un jeu de lumières, de formes et de transparences, l'architecte prend le pas sur le mouvement futuriste, en une anticipation d'une grande pureté.

L'attività mondana derivante dalla posizione politica del proprietario di questa casa fece sì che, in primo luogo, venisse espressa ad Horta l'esigenza di difenderne l'intimità. La facciata, di pietra calcarea bianca, presenta uno schema compositivo in cui prevalgono le linee orizzontali, che conferiscono all'edificio equilibrio statico. Senza dubbio, la facciata posteriore esprime grande vivacità espressiva da parte dell'architetto. Fu concepita con grande coerenza e rigoroso razionalismo, come si può ben apprezzare nella soluzione che abilmente si diede alle piccole scale che permettono il passaggio della luce al livello interrato. Si può pero anche scoprire un Horta dalle fantasie quasi futuriste, che disegna finestre di cristallo, di forme fantasiose, al di sopra della "bow window". All'interno, è doveroso segnalare la scala, che costituisce il principale elemento attorno a cui si articola la composizione. Il problema del riscaldamento viene risolto attraverso l'introduzione di alcuni signolari caloriferi che seguono la planimetria delle bucature. In questo gioco di luci, forme e trasparenze, l'architetto anticiperà il movimento futurista, con delle soluzioni di singolare purezza.

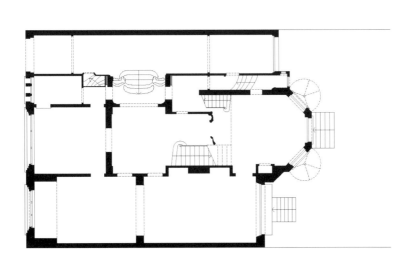

Plan
Grundriss
Niveau
Pianta

0 1 2

Max Hallet House **59**

Waucquez Shopping Mall

Rue des Sables 20, Brusseles, Belgium
1903–1906

This building is the only one that remains from the so-called Victor Horta golden age. But even if the interiors have been lightly modified, the façade has remained unchanged. Horta combines, in this front, which is slightly concave, a seven-windowed rhythm to mark the central character of the composition as a whole. Hence, we see a return to the large stone arches he had used in the House of the People. The columns here are also of stone, which contributes to the generation of a solid look, one of great figurative mastery. They are also accompanied by two brackets one over the door and the other over the window. The intention of the architect to establish a language of his own is also appreciable in the curvature of the façade itself, which breaks with the topography of the site and assigns a certain monumentality to the work. Inside the building, an oversize skylight framed in steel serves as a central distributing element for the interior space. The whole blends the functional and the monumental. It is a building that initiates the architect's perhaps least innovative period, a time when he goes back to the classical tradition, which he evokes and uses with great mastery.

Dieses Warenhaus ist das einzige noch bestehende aus dem sogenannten goldenen Zeitalter Hortas und obwohl sein Inneres leicht verändert wurde, blieb die Fassade intakt und erhalten. Horta kombinierte auf der Vorderseite in leicht konkavem Rhythmus sieben Fenster, welche einen zentralen Platz in der Komposition einnehmen. Auf diese Weise kehrt er zu den großen Steinbögen zurück, die er bereits in anderen Werken wie dem Volkshaus anwendete. Die solide wirkenden Stützpfeiler sind ebenfalls aus Stein und zeugen von großer figurativer Meisterschaft. Sie werden an ihren Enden von zwei Konsolen abgeschlossen, eine über der Tür und eine über dem Fenster. Der Wille des Architekten, seine eigene Sprache einzubringen, zeigt sich auch in der Krümmung der Fassade, die der Form des Grundstücks entgegengesetzt ist und dem Werk etwas Monumentales verleiht. Im Inneren dominiert ein mit Glas und Metall überdachtes Oberlicht und bildet das zentrale Element. Die Einheit kombiniert Monumentalität mit Zweckmäßigkeit und leitete eine weniger innovative Phase des Architekten ein, in der er die Tendenz zeigte, die klassische Tradition mit großer Meisterschaft auferstehen und vorherrschen zu lassen.

Ces grands magasins sont les seuls subsistant de l'âge d'or de Horta et, bien que les intérieurs en aient été modifié légèrement, la façade a été préservée intacte. Horta combine sur la façade, légèrement concave, le rythme des sept fenêtres avec le caractère central de la composition. Il revient ainsi aux grands arches de pierre précédemment employés pour des œuvres comme la Maison du Peuple. Les piliers sont également en pierre, contribuant à générer un aspect solide et une grande maîtrise figurative, et sont coiffés aux extrêmes par deux encorbellements – l'un sur la porte et l'autre sous la fenêtre. L'intention de l'architecte, établir son propre langage, se fait manifeste dans la courbure de cette façade, en rupture avec la forme du terrain et apportant un caractère monumental à l'œuvre. À l'intérieur, un puit de lumière couvert par un toit en verrière et en métal régit la distribution du bâtiment et devient l'élément central. L'ensemble marie fonctionnalité et monumentalité tout en initiant une étape de la carrière de l'architecte, moins innovante et tendant plutôt à faire prévaloir la tradition classique, évoquée et utilisée magistralement.

Questi grandi magazzini sono gli unici che ci sono rimasti della cosiddetta età dell'oro di Horta e, sebbene gli interni siano stati modificati in ristrettezze, la facciata si è mantenuta intatta. Horta articola nel fronte, leggermente concavo, il ritmo di sette finestre, secondo uno schema compositivo centrale. In questo modo ritorna ai grandi archi di pietra che aveva già utilizzato in opere come la Casa del Popolo. Anche i pilastri sono di pietra, fatto questo che contribuisce a generare un aspetto solido e di grande capacità figurativa, e sono lavorati agli estemi con due mensole, una sopra la porta e una sopra la finestra. L'intenzione dell'architetto di definire un linguaggio personale si apprezza anche nella curvatura della facciata, che rompe con la forma del lotto ed apporta monumentalità alla costruzione. All'interno, un pozzo di luce coperto da un tetto di vetro e metallo determina la distribuzione dell'edificio e ne configura l'elemento centrale. L'insieme accosta funzionalità e monumentalità ed inizia il periodo meno innovatore dell'attività dell'architetto, con già una tendenza a far prevalere la tradizione classica, evocata ed utilizzata con grande maestria.

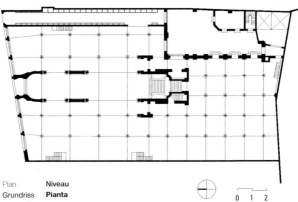

Plan   Niveau
Grundriss   **Pianta**

0 1 2

Brugmann Hospital

Place Van Gehucthen 4, Brussels, Belgium
1906–1923

When he accepted the commission to build the new hospital that was to replace the old buildings of the Saint-Jean and Saint-Pierre, Horta was forced to adapt himself to a trapezoidal plot with a curvilinear base. The work took seventeen years, and during this time various modifications were effected in the initial plan. But in spite of the war and the related controversies, Horta brings about the revelation of a new side to his own architectural personality. In this process, and regardless of the limits imposed by the modest means available, his mastery emerges. Horta chose a horizontal distribution that motivated a certain critical commentary, something he defends himself against in his "Memoirs" with an essential argument: the Brugmann Hospital, with its horizontality, will acquire a more human dimension within the oversize terrain available, doing so, moreover, more economically. The complex links small modules of great chromatic and volumetric variety under the lemma of symmetry, the architect's most characteristic feature. Following this work, Horta will be not only the architect of the bourgeoisie, but also an architect open to other European influences, one of social opening and urban dimension.

Bei dem Auftrag zu einem neuen Krankenhaus, das die alten Gebäude von Saint-Jean und Saint-Pierre ersetzen sollte, musste Horta sich mit einem trapezförmigen Grundstück und einer bogenförmigen Basis auseinandersetzen. Die Arbeiten dauerten 17 Jahre und es wurden verschiedene Veränderungen in Bezug auf das Anfangsprojekt vorgenommen. Trotz des Krieges und etlicher Kontroversen gelang es Horta, eine neue Facette seiner architektonischen Persönlichkeit zu zeigen, in der, trotz der Beschränkung auf bescheidene Mittel, seine ganze Meisterschaft hervorsticht. Horta wählte eine horizontale Aufteilung, die verschiedentlich Kritik hervorrief, aber von ihm in seinen „Memoiren" mit einem wesentlichen Argument verteidigt wurde: Das Brugmann-Krankenhaus erhält durch diese horizontale Ausrichtung auf dem ausgedehnten Grundstück eine menschlichere Dimension, einmal ganz abgesehen von der Kostenersparnis. Der Komplex verbindet kleine farblich und in Bezug auf das Volumen vielfältig erstellte Module mit dem Ziel der Symmetrie, dem typischen Kennzeichen des Architekten. Nach diesem Werk wurde Horta nicht mehr nur als der Architekt des Bürgertums gesehen, sondern als ein für die Einflüsse Europas offener Architekt mit sozialer Ader und städteplanerischer Dimension.

En acceptant de construire le nouvel hôpital remplaçant les anciens bâtiments de Saint-Jean et Saint-Pierre, Horta dut s'adapter à un terrain trapézoïdal à la base curviligne. Les travaux allaient durer dix-sept ans et voir diverses modifications en regard du projet initial. Cependant, malgré la guerre et les controverses suscitées, Horta réussit à révéler une nouvelle facette de sa personnalité architectonique au travers de laquelle, bien que limité par des moyens modestes, toute sa maîtrise se fait manifeste. Horta choisit une distribution horizontale qui motiveraient diverses critiques, dont il se défendit dans ses « Mémoires » avec un argument essentiel : l'Hôpital Brugmann acquiert, en raison de son horizontalité, une dimension plus humaine sur un terrain étendu, tout en proposant un projet plus économique. Le complexe réunit de petits modules d'une grande variété chromatique et volumétrique sous le signe de la symétrie, trait caractéristique de l'architecte. Après cette œuvre, Horta n'est plus seulement l'architecte de la bourgeoisie mais s'ouvre aux influences européennes, conscient socialement et de dimension urbaine.

Accettando di costruire il nuovo ospedale che sarebbe andato a sostituire gli antichi edifici di Saint-Jean e Saint-Pierre, Horta dovette adattarsi ad un lotto trapezoidale e con base curvilinea. Il cantiere durò diciassette anni, nei quali si ebbero diverse modifiche rispetto al progetto iniziale. Senza dubbio, nonostante la guerra ed i problemi insorti, Horta riesce in questo caso ad esprimere un nuovo aspetto della sua personalità architettonica in cui, sia pur condizionato dalla modestia dei mezzi a disposizione, emerge una eccezionale bravura. Horta scelse una distribuzione orizzontale che provocò diverse critiche, dalle quali si difese nelle sue "Memorie" con una argomentazione essenziale: l'Ospedale Brugmann acquisisce, con la sua orizzontalità, una dimensione più umana all'interno di un lotto gigantesco, oltre evidentemente a definire un progetto sensibilmente più economico. Il complesso unisce piccoli moduli di grande varietà cromatica e volumetrica sotto il principio della simmetria, carattere tipico dell'architetto. Con questa opera, Horta non solo si afferma come l'architetto della borghesia, ma anche come un architetto aperto alle influenze europee, di apertura sociale e dimensione urbana.

Plan **Niveau**
Grundriss **Pianta**

0 1 2

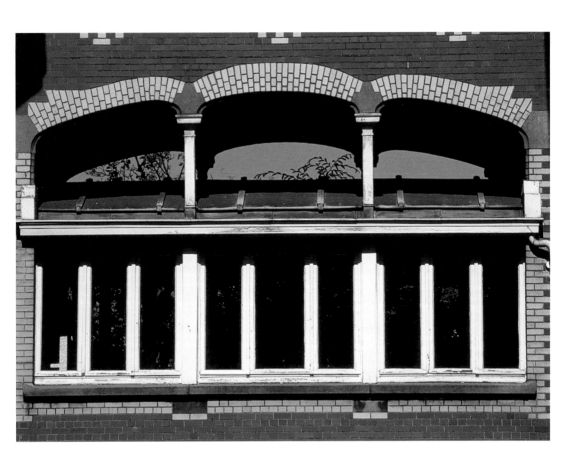

Chronology of Horta's works

1861	Birth in Ghent, Belgium, January 6.
1873	Enters the Department of Architecture of the Academy of Fine Arts, Ghent, Belgium.
1878	Works with the architect Jules Debuysson, Montmartre, Paris, France.
1880	Moves to Brussels.
1881–1884	Studies at the Academy of Fine Arts, Brussels, Belgium.
1884	Begins to work with Alphonse Balat, architect to Leopold II of Belgium.
	Wins the Godecharle Competition with the design of the Parliament Building, Brussels, Belgium.
1885	Builds his first work, Geenens House, Ghent, Belgium.
	Wins the competition held by the Museum of Natural History, Brussels, Belgium.
1889	Shares with Guillaume Charlier the prize for the monument to the painter Louis Gallait, Tournai, Belgium.
1890	Design for the rehabilitation of the Salle des Fêtes de la Madeleine, Brussels, Belgium.
1893	Wins tenured full professorship in architecture at the University of Brussels, Belgium.
1893–1895	Autrique House, Brussels, Belgium.
	Tassel House, Brussels, Belgium.
1894–1896	Winssinger House, Brussels, Belgium.
	Frison House, Brussels, Belgium.
1894–1898	Solvay House, Brussels, Belgium.
1895	Kindergarten on the rue Saint-Ghislain, Brussels, Belgium.
1895–1901	Van Eetvelde House, Brussels, Belgium.
1895–1897	Deprez House, Brussels, Belgium.
1896	Solvay Laboratories, Brussels, Belgium.
1897	Timberman Country House, Uccle, Belgium.
	Named extraordinary professor at the University of Brussels, Belgium.
1898–1901	Horta Studio/House, Brussels, Belgium. (Now the Horta Museum)
	House of the People, Brussels, Belgium. (No longer standing)
1899	Les Epinglettes country house for Maurice Frison, Uccle, Belgium.
	Design for the Maternity Pavilion for Œuvre Sainte-Anne for the 1900 World Exposition in Paris, France.
	Aubecq House, Brussels, Belgium.
1900	Furnémont Country House, Uccle, Belgium.

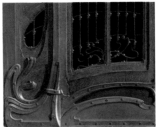

	Interior design for the Dapsens House, Brussels, Belgium.
1901	Roger Residence, Brussels, Belgium.
	House and studio for the sculptor Pierre Braecke, Brussels, Belgium.
	House and studio for the sculptor Fernand Dubois, Forest, Belgium.
1903–1905	Max Hallet House, Brussels, Belgium.
1903	First plans for the Museum of Fine Arts of Tournai, Belgium.
1903–1906	Waucquez Shopping Mall, Brussels, Belgium.
1905	Villa Fernand Dubois, Sosoye, Belgium.
1906	First designs for the Brugmann Hospital, Brussels, Belgium.
1907	J. Hiclet Stores, Brussels, Belgium.
1909	Cazier Residence, Ixelles, Belgium.
	Wolfers Stores, Brussels, Belgium.
1910	House for Dr. Terwagne, Amberes, Belgium.
1911	Resigns from his tenured professorship in architecture at the University of Brussels, Belgium.
	Absalon Stores, Brussels, Belgium.
	Wiener Residence, Brussels, Belgium.
1912	First designs for the Central Railroad Station, Brussels, Belgium.
	Country house for himself, La Bastide in La Hulpe, Belgium.
1913–1915	Named director of the Academy of Fine Arts, Brussels, Belgium.
1915–1918	Moves to the United States and leaves the presidency of the Academy of Fine Arts of Brussels, Belgium.
1920	First designs for the Palace of Fine Arts in Brussels, Belgium.
1923	Medical-Surgical Institute Cinquantenaire, Brussels, Belgium.
	Inauguration of the Brugmann Hospital, Brussels, Belgium.
1927	Resumes the position of president of the Academy of Fine Arts, Brussels, Belgium.
1928	Inauguration of the Palace of Fine Arts, Brussels, Belgium, and the Museum of Fine Arts, Tournai, Belgium.
1929	Projects for the reconstruction of two primary schools and a kindergarten, Brussels, Belgium.
1931	Retires from the Academy of Fine Arts of Brussels.
1932	King Albert I of Belgium decorates Horta with the title of baron.
1937	Final design for the Central Railroad Station of Brussels, Belgium.
1941	Publishes his "Memoirs".
1945	Destroys part of his files and drawings.
1947	Death, September 7; cremated in the cemetery at Ixelles, Belgium.